HOW TO STOP SCHOOL & MASS SHOOTINGS; DEAR PARENTS

By Hitachi Choparazzi

Acknowledgements

All the victims from massive shootings throughout the world. Also to all the loved ones, family, and friends of the victims. May the Creator of the universe bless you all with peace during the healing and grieving process, and the strength to rebuild your lives with forward progress always. Each day is a struggle. However, a loss is not always a total loss, it's a way to learn lessons, strengths, and see other blessings, reasons, and seasons in life. I wrote this for y'all.

ATTN:

This is a public prevention book for social awareness, mental health, self-development, and self-awareness. This book is from the author's perspective as a prevention analysis, advocate, parent. Using all the data, research, patterns, learnt behavior, and psychographic to put this book into a better perspective for parents and people globally to read and share the message of prevention and awareness of each parent being held responsible to hold their kids accountable at a young age initiating from the home. Avoiding neglect, catching triggers, detecting mental illness, and evolving parenting skills.

This book is not an intention to mislead you that all massive and school shootings will immediately stop after reading it. It's simply to all the parents as a prevention in their home for their kids to avoid behavior patterns, bad habits, neglect, bullying, cyber influences that lead to massive media shootings or suicide.

I wrote this book manual handwritten to take the time out dedicated to the lives lost in massive shootings and to prevent others from losing their lives. It may prevent and save multiple people and massive lives that matter. Or by you reading this to help spread awareness and save your own children or others' lives, too. Thank you all. God bless. Please share the message from one parent to the other parent. To touch more and reach more, we can definitely prevent more.

Contents

FOREWORD

Nowadays school shootings and massive shootings have become the new norm in a digital era worldwide, but increasingly in numbers in the U.S.

As I was sitting down to manually handwrite this book, I was saddened by yet another school shooting in Santa Clarita, California, high school, with multiple students shot and a few fatal, which only took 16 seconds for the student that was allegedly bullied to carry out before turning the gun on himself. This marked the 30th school shooting in 2019 by mid-November.

Which is becoming so commonplace, along with people showing up in public areas for acts of massive shootings to carry out for a public display of hurt and casualties. People's ill will to inflict pain and harm, which is digital and media-driven to audiences globally.

The latest school shooting was a short segment of breaking news, that's how such a new normal it has become in our American society. 80 percent were bullied, 81 percent suffered mental illness, and 80 percent indicated they were going to act out the shootings. It will always be a sign or long record of shooter's profile and their behaviors. Signs of drug use, depression, self-harm, or mental health. All stemming from childhood, which is number-one psychologist based for prolific shifts of ill will, predatory behaviors, and acts of violence. I will show you how to reduce and recognize in scope.

Schools and communities never think it will happen with them. Parents never think it's going to happen with their kid. However, I disagree and believe it starts in the home from the beginning, and parents being all held accountable. To further engage, monitor, and teach kids. Enable to avoid from neglect, disengagement, bad triggers that spiral them into negativity, cognitive issues, self-doubt, and hate. Parents need to look deeper, open up dialogue, have awareness of all child's time, online and video games usage, also people and things they associate with. Intervention is key and a tool in prevention.

Proper preparation prevents poor performances and tragedies, which all starts within the home and every parent fully engaged to child, despite work and social life. Don't let the new digital era and social new norms raise your kids. This is a prevention book solution. I'll teach you how to engage proactively, tactics, strategies, tips, and message for proper prevention to spread one home and kid at a time. All kids' lives matter.

- Chapter 1 -

"Dear Parents"

Dear parents, I open up the first chapter of this book dedicated to all of you. Single parents, same-sex parents, adoptive parents, and grandparents playing parent or foster parents are all included. My aim is to upgrade, bring awareness, push more home effort, time, monitoring, and love in the home. With effective solutions, tips, strategies of proper prevention and how to spot triggers, mental illness, behavior patterns, bullying, negative social influences, body language and everything in between.

I believe the best way to stop a massive shooting or a school shooting is a proper prevention method that starts in the home from the inception of the child. Every parent must be held accountable for their child and household. This book is not an aim attacking your parenting skills. It's simply to help you with awareness of new times and social norms that our kids are going thru in this new digital era that we did not have to go thru and catch all the signs before they spiral out of control and snowball effect where it grows on the child, teen or adulthood into a boiling point, erupting like an active volcano, lashing out, inflicting trauma on self or others. Suicide prevention, all before it's too late, which all parents blame themselves and live with guilt on their conscience of knowing the fact they could've done better and took the time out to investigate, monitor, and help their child. Also saving others and students that never had a real chance at life awes and to grow.

With all the new social norms and platforms, most kids and adults take on an identity crisis and pressure they deal with daily. They are simply confused and feeding into others' social profiles, feeds, and norms. Taking on their digital identify from their social page and profile. Then they actually start to believe that virtual reality is their norm reality. Just like augmented reality, it's superimposed on the kids and adults, which further influences them to become all that they see and hear in the digital world. Even the gaming is influential, especially all the shooting warfare games. Kids attach to that and alter their consciousness to eventually act out on it. Instant gratification and desired reward cravings force them to act out on impulse and rewire the brain to the extreme, which push it into reality. The brain does not differentiate reality from artificial, it just produces whatever story you feed it or desire to seek as your reality to be true.

This is why President Donald Trump stated it is because of the video game usage, which, I think, it's a factor definitely, but not the whole blame on massive shooting like he claims. Gaming could be played responsibly with the wrong influential shooting game, it can have not dire effects if the individual is competent and in a good health space.

As parents we tend to give up on being hands-on at a certain point once the child can walk, talk, eat, and be co-independent. Also our focal point is not directed and engaged more with our children after that baby stage. Then we go into a provide, safety, and educational phase, which we feel the only job is to provide food, shelter, make sure the kids are enrolled into school and are safe well-being and health environment with little to no engagement true interactions with the kids or teens. The majority of parents are caught up in work life and fighting an intense balance dealing with time and financial, not realizing that we are leaving open ends to other levels of parenting, especially in this new digital era. Everything is sensitive and enhanced.

You have to close in these gaps to advance as an effective prevention tool. A huge problem is trust with the kids and teens. Parents trust them to do the right things and behave. However, parents do not reinforce or try to reform in their kids' lives. Also now the kids and teens don't trust the parents and adults in the home because they simply feel that the parents cannot relate to their problems, pressures, and too outdated. The kids say the parents don't understand their generation.

This is where a dialogue needs to be opened and really the ability to understand, engage, and listen to kids' needs, behavior, and social patterns. You have to collaborate together to fix and problem solve. You need to know your kids and teens further or simply get hip and know the new them and social logics they grew into or realities they became.

You must not force your way into their new space they have grown into or try to force conversations and engagement, creating awkwardness between them. Kids don't articulate nowadays how we did as we were that same age. Kids starting at 10 years of age start texting and develop an anti-social behavior mechanism. They can be in the same house and room and will rather prefer to text message you. So you cannot force your way into their space and expect them to talk, share feelings, and engage. You have to earn and reestablish their real trust. Really learn them, their new habits, follow their new patterns. Probing around their room and personal space will not help, they will just continue to block you out further. You need to be conscious of this and how to develop tactics to inner probe without them feel like you are crossing and overstepping boundaries.

The goal is prevention to be proactive, not reactive, to the kids and things in the household. Intervention and to integrate as a prevention curriculum remedy. I will show you why and how to problem solve and troubleshoot in this prevention awareness book. Social development is key.

Please, do not passively engage with your kids or prevention. Reassess kids' well-being, stress, and anxiety. Focus on giving and in a realm where you help proactively of what's going on in your kids' life or with everyone. Go around and practice this thru technique. Have complete structure of your kids' lives beyond average or what you used to. Instead challenge yourself to come at a totally new different angle and be open-minded. Develop better relationships and communication skills to believe in them. Respect is established and how you talk to them is very direct, which also affects them, so do not down-talk them with negativity for them to actualize and play into that. Their egos flare up and they attack and lash out from hurt or defensive because they do not know how to handle certain responses and interactions. Attach to the structures versus the outcome or keep your mind attached to them. It is easy for kids to sink into their own world with these devices, etc., nowadays. Kids become bored and disillusioned from school, especially hyperlinked thinkers. Social norms influence them and behaviors because they want to be accepted. Seeking validation from others and the world wide web versus parents and family. Desire behavior is the norm behavior. Society leans on them all, peer pressure, cyber pressure, idolization, and popularity contest. Most likes and shares, and so on.

Have kids join groups they love and inspire them to want to be or do. Learning new things, words, and hands-on development. Kids connect with groups and shared context. Social groups you view ways and how you interpret, work together, and problem solve. Teens can always use a change before adulthood to help with their transformation. Expectation of norms, too, can be pressure to them and introverts kids, too.

They figuring out that journey to authentic self. It is human nature to follow the path of the masses. Kids are outcasted behind the mask, a misfit, or person trying to fit in the world as they go with all the trends. Like a mirror neuron theory, your brain reacts to the belief system, then deflects what they see. Desire to reach the excesses of the imagination. They will fight to the death of who they are. They sat there watching characters that kids defined themselves against different tolerance, popular beliefs. Behavior immediate rewards.

Playing, singing, reading, and writing are main traits in development. Pay attention to them in school and monitor their progress or social disengagements. Increase observability. No excuses, eliminating all excuses. You can even have a daily monitor and increasing engagement checklist to get you started to develop a new habit of proper prevention. Your kid can even suffer from impulsive control or anger management. Mental health can trigger at any time or stages in life. Most people doubt their kid can suffer from mental illness because they never pay attention to the triggers or change of behavior because their child did not have it as an infant. However, that is not facts and parents need to do their due diligence. Observations, not being in denial. Research online, other communities with same symptoms your child suffers from. Do not be ashamed or embarrassed to reach out or tap into resources and doctors to get your child correct mental health evaluations and help. It may save their and others' lives. Medicine is not the solution all the time for everybody. However, some people suffering from mental illness need it. If you still not comfortable with seeking help for your child that's troubled, you can always Google certain traits, actions, behaviors, patterns, and symptoms. Please, as a parent, do not be selfish, be selfless for your kids or teens so they do not carry them same problems and traits into adulthood to figure out on their own. So, again, please reach out and get them the proper help needed or recommended.

Make mental notes of kids' signs, body language, and demeanors. You need to be a realist in these new change of times. Also a lot not always mental defects, some start mental blow-up thru mental neglect. Most parents can catch if agile. You need to keep that edge of awareness of your kids and teens. If you feel like your job as a parent is already too hard and too much distress with teens that do not listen and out of control, you can always seek help with other family, friends, groups, and organizations before it's too late, also.

Thru the lenses of the world, kids see and become their attitude or amplitude of mocking others for themselves. Young people need to mold a vision of themselves to become an asset versus public liability. It is designed to destroy sense of self.

Parents, remember kids think and let other people or social public opinions be their reality or shape it. Stop the kids in their tracks and interrupt their story, then dismantle their current belief into a large influence and inspire their heart for them to be motivated to make better choices. Also to pursue.

Please consider and take in all my advice and do not assume you know your kids. Learn and study them to be able to transform them and impact them with new techniques and strategies to help and move them.

Parents must first remember they taught their kids what the kids actually know, not what all the parents actually know as parents and adults.

Parents must speak from head and heart, not the same scripted speech where your kids...they know, they know, and finish your sentence before you or simultaneously. You must extract the problem from kids and replace with your energy.

Please, learn to recognize when your kids are troubled or in a dark place and bring them back to the light and life. Then transform how they think of themselves and life. All they doing is going thru transitional stage of life, trying to figure their way and discover what works and their authentic self. This task is so hard nowadays versus your childhood generation with the new wave of digital footprints and distraction on a highly competitive. All kids feel like they are truly one viral video away from being famous, which also imprints negative and collectively on their psyche, altering their mind frame for validation seek direct attention, popularity, and instant gratification. This is where their young egos form and built on negative resentment, thoughts, and cravings. This is what we need to spot and be aware of when the kids are negatively impacted, influenced, bullied, or feeling suicidal, which more people commit suicide, over 3K more than accidents. However, 80 percent is preventable with help and talking people out of it by calming them down as a solution.

If we multiply the voice of hope, awareness, accountability, it can be the proper prevention steps inquired to take, which it definitely reduces negativity, bullying, tragedy, and suicide rates. Evil prevails once people do not care, nor take the time out and being self-centered. You cannot have a to-each-its-own mentality and neglect your responsibility and obligation to your kids and kids of the community in order to do a proactively push this prevention, starting one household at a time while spreading the message wholeheartedly that can save multiple lives and massive shooting from actually occurring. That's why I sat down to write.

- Chapter 2 -

"Neglect"

Neglect is the main focal point because it is the number one problem where it initiates, which leads to problematic children, teens, and behaviors. Indirectly, most parents neglect their child; this same neglect leads to the void. Next the gap of the child attempting to fill in the void, attached is all the social behavior, pressure, influence, drug abuse, or bullying and so on.

The problem can be fixed from parents stop tending to kids and neglect their full responsibility until they turn 18 years old. Do not neglect your kids, instead engage more with them. Please, do not let social media and YouTube raise them. People do not realize they emancipate their children at young age to gaming, edevices, etc., all to influence and shape their perceptions into new personality and streaming digital identity and digital footprints as cyber rock stars or misfits in new generation.

This neglect is an important basis because even as a parent, we become busy and lack being hands-on like we did when they were babies. You give your kids space to allow them to figure things out for themselves and to hone and develop their own problem-solving skills. However, how much space is neglected to where you have created a distance? Or this distance between you and the child created a dent and sinkhole or a black hole? It could be extremely detrimental. This is exactly what you as a parent need to be aware and conscious of. You cannot simply see your kid on a tablet and think they simply playing or out of your way. You need to check their content on that tablet and guard them just like you did when they were infants. Monitoring content, time, and usage is mandatory. You cannot care about them being mad at you, they will get over it or keep pushing you until you break back into your old ways. Kids look for your gaps to push you to relapse and go back on your words of discipline. You need to remember you are the parents and it's your job to help, protect, and guide them correctly. You not their friend or classmate. Even if you are a passive laidback parent and your child is more of an introvert, it still needs to be boundaries, rules, laws, and non-negotiable discipline. If you set terms, you must stick and abide by them versus neglecting them. Kids are very smart, adaptive, and will test your firmness and boundaries, especially with timing when you not around or at work. Whereas, timing is everything and kids definitely know this and use it to their advantage as a tool to overcome your obstacle you set as boundaries and timelines for them.

Now, if the question you're asking yourself is "Am I truly neglecting my kids?" or "How can I do a better job with engagement and prevention?" then you definitely need to step up further and pay attention to the useful tips, methods, and strategies of new angles of awareness and proactive prevention of engagement initiating from the home early on before it's catastrophic and too late to fix.

This cause for commitment, no excuses, period. Work is no excuse, time is no excuse, and fatigue is no excuse. Every kid's life matters and you not just saving your own kid's life, you are saving other people's kids' lives, too. Most kids hold each other accountable of their actions if you responsibly bestow that into them. You have to be willing to challenge yourself and set new standards. You must throw out your old teaching and parenting habits and create new ones.

This is all framework and tools to be aware, engage, and connect further as a parent. 99 percent of parents is doing their best job, so please do not defend or disregard your parenting or shame your kids or exploit their vulnerability. It's simply to be open and aware to try to implement a new prevention method and challenge yourself to step up and start activating new prevention strategies.

The question now is, where do you start and how do you start? If you are really looking at your child or teen thinking it's too late, well, you are definitely wrong. It is never too late. Minor damage can be fixed and your kid can still get the proper alignment and influence to do a turnaround on the straight path. It cannot hurt to help, reassess, then intervene their wrong actions and behavior patterns.

Remember if you go into this with an open mind to the new ideal method of proper prevention and set your mind to an imminent change, then challenge yourself to evolve, that's when you will see positive results, reactions, and a new dialogue with your kids or teen with a new level of trust and engagement into their new generation space and time.

To change the narrative, you change your story/actions. It's the story you tell yourself by observing the narrative and focusing on the actual narrative you must retrace, rewrite your own narrative perspective of your new way of formulating your parenting skills to fix it versus neglect or psychotherapy.

Convert your pain to power, your neglect to prevention, being hands-on diligent, aware, and very observant of your children's behavior switch and pattern, which will set off red flags or silent alarms in your head soon as you see it to evaluate the situation, feelings, distress, or temperament, which again allows you to train to see the gaps. Therefore further engagement will lead to comfort, trust, and your kid or teen to open up to you about what's bothering them or ongoing issues and bullying they may not feel comfortable at first or otherwise discussing with a parent about. Nowadays the kids really feel like the parents are lost and cannot relate to their pain, life, or understand what they going thru because they are too busy parenting with an iron fist and neglecting what the kids' mental state and mood is. Typically parents at this stage just worry about the basics, like their children following all their typical rules of chorus, going to school, and don't get into trouble or the parents' face and way. If you are one of those typical parents, you must evolve, change your standard status quo of the masses. You have to really be so driven and dedicated, too, else all falls down the mental neglect aisle with your children.

Step up and start new strategies. Your kid's life is not at stake, so do not make them feel worthless. This is to simply show you a way to connect. Things or parents contaminate the kids' minds of how to think, what to be, and their standards. You have to deconstruct as a parent and the generational template. Be careful of what you put in your kid's mind and first foundation. Kids feel shame and guilty if they do not live into same parents' mindset, fit into their same shoes, or follow their standard footsteps of pressure. Decision making is solely up to your children to make the best and right choices.

No one wants to be uncomfortable or neglected. Vulnerability, risk, uncertainty, and not knowing weighs heavy on teens, which emotional behavior and impulse is not looked at as courage and brave, further hitting and consuming them with shame and further vulnerability stages.

As parents do not forget how to discover the signs or interact, connect, and socialization. Be held accountable to not just your own children, but the neighbors and community if you see any red flag warnings. Please notify the other kids' parents of their kids being troubled or affected in any way of behavior changes out the ordinary.

Bullying is crucial and one of the most prolific triggers to send kids off edge sooner or later in life. This one is often tricky because the kids being bullied outside or in school mask it well in front of parents, teachers, and others. However, if you very observant of your children, checking in on them daily and probing more, even when they are lying and hiding these issues, then you can see thru all their dishonest dialogue and their mood switch, anxiety, depression states, and troubleshoot to make them reveal what toxic environment or element pulling on them.

Bullying can lead to retaliation, just like being bullied by a certain ethnic group can lead to racial attention. Never connected or communicated with that community besides be bullied or racial bias from others, which leads to hate crimes, hatred motivated and influenced or driven, also called Pulse shootings. Have to come out someday or manifest some way and progress like a cancer cell, then explode with deadly devastation of rage that could've all been prevented from inception of the home in early years on.

Therefore, are you neglecting looking for patterns, behavior changes in kids and teens? Also signs to prevent acts of violence and spiral massive or school shootings?

See, when you think there is no neglect in your home or it won't happen in your home or neighborhood, you are not being open to suggestive framework or constructive criticism by no means. Again, you need to understand neglect further. It's not you merely neglecting your duty as a parent or neglect like child abandonment. You must not neglect to go the extra mile and evolve your mind and parenting methods dealing with new times and this new social media, digital era. Kids and teens are way more advanced and develop new traits thru peers, trends, and good influencers or detrimental influencers. Also class bullying, neighborhood bullies, and cyber bullies. The question to really ask yourself, are you a hundred percent that right now you are aware of all your kids' new and old habits? Along with your teens' transitional phases trying to find themselves and authentic nature? Then with a proper preventive tool? Or do you honestly feel you are at that level of engagement with your children? Without no change? Even if you are a hundred percent confident you are at that place and know and trust your child, how will you identify when they change to another level? Usually at this morphing stage, they transform still with that same innocent smile and regular engagement that you used to. These kids and teens are great at masking themselves to mislead and even lie direct to their parents always. So therefore, the kids and teens all evolved, so why haven't you and the parents?

We learn patterns, behaviors that come in our lives. Cue triggers and responses or connecting triggers. Parents monitor, engage, and check, not neglect. Check frequently all your child's or teen's content and social media engagement.

A lot of kids, teens, people have posted publicly their outrage, cry for help beforehand. Copycat syndromes of need for direct attention cause them to inflict pain for an immediate dire impact. This all could be prevented and stopped or caught beforehand. Usually that person suffered from neglect of not just the community or world, but the actualization of the beginning stages at the very home that individual transpired from. A lot of people and parents wish they can go back and wonder where did they go wrong at and live with guilty remorse with the weight of the world hanging over their backs. This book is to prevent you from becoming that same parent who suffering to this day. Let's please start by one parent and household at a time. From parent-to-parent dialogue to spread proper prevention and come together to help build, heal, and share info to troubleshoot.

How to fix it, heal, and mend, how to deal with bottled-in emotions. How to find positive and good from it. And so much more is all the parenting and community dialogue that needs to be open, dealing with neglect and your responsibility to further catch your children or teens behavior patterns, dishonesty, and when they are troubled by something to connect and help them by problem solving techniques. This is how we all as parents can do better and get better as a whole and save our children and the neighbors, too.

Now for all the parents dealing with a loss and living with remorse, hurt, or regret, even grief, must keep vision of future progress that draws enthusiasm and growth. Transform lower energy into higher energy. Define positive and connect with it, like being stronger to decide to teach you something or do something for somebody or the world. Even if it's just compassion and gratitude. When you spread and share the love to others going thru similar loss or grief, it helps to heal, rebuild, and mend broken areas. You can even do little as to share links, videos, quotes, and inspirational energy of the day.

Intensity, brutal, and hurt will pass over and change in time, just as a storm does. Even if you coming out of a depression, make a move and goal daily. It could be as simple as a shower, reading, writing, or listening to mantra Audibles. Most of the time neglect, anger, or depression is coming from a hurt place, displacement, and poor management of the mind. So remember, neglect on both ends as a parent and as a child can lead to insurmountable problems, meaning too big and out of control.

- Chapter 3 -

"Social Norms & Influences"

In this chapter of social norms and influences, we will address some ongoing influences and tackle how the new social norms in a digital space is the new wave trend that acts like an algorithm to every child or teen engaging on social platforms. Then I will give you effective tools, tips, and strategies to spot and stop them with a different parenting approach method to implement. All with daily practice a new prevention system and method until it will become adaptable part of your behavior after repetition into a habitual norm.

Let's start with influences. Influencers good or bad can definitely move or inspire your child or teen to react positive or negative. This also can be so easily ignored or overlooked because parents may think their child is just on YouTube watching creative content or videos or even on social media socializing with their peers, never seeing the underlying problematic or confrontational issue.

This all needs to be noticed and parents very observant because at this point is the kids' cue shift where they are easily misled and still soak up everything like an actual sponge, same as they did since day one with sensory as an infant.

Yes, parents, your kids can pick up traits from influencers and copycat influencers' ideal identity. This is because usually of the influencer's platform or audience that the kids and teens want or seek for validation, fame, love, or social acceptance. It could also be from pressure in this new digital era. Pressure from their peers, classmates, or relatives. Even neglect can be a trigger cause for them to gravitate and idolize influencers.

This all pushes the youth to run to rush and find a place for a digital footprint to imprint and be heard. Therefore, if a teen is seriously trolling and leaving hate comments all over the internet, they can seriously be hurting, neglected, bullying, or parents too time-consumed to further probe and engage as well, which will spiral downhill and take on a snowball effect. If your children and teens are not being held accountable or to a behavioral standard daily.

You must engage with your kids and guard their daily content online, music, and even their socializing background. Like their peers, classmates, and neighbors all can influence them good or bad. Most of all very quickly just to be accepted or have likes and comments online. It definitely is a different beast to tackle nowadays because instead of kids being open books and honest, the new Generation Z is way more introverted and very anti-social. It is way harder to break through to them. It's up to you to decide who comes over to see them, engage, or where they spend the night at and what classmates are safe influencers with good vibes, energy being positive versus bring your children down or negativity affecting them.

To select what is a good influencer versus a bad influencer is not an easy job as you may think because the internet especially is a never-ending space. You cannot catch all the bad influences your kids pick up. However, you can pick up sign from your kids' behavior, patterns, new habits such as talking different, dressing different, or even listening to vulgar music with video games that alter their identity. You'll know when your kids do this drastic change almost 95 percent of the time. All of them try to mask themselves, but as the parents you must see thru that mask and address them, calling them and their new actions out loud. Some kids just need an adult to catch them when they falling down the wrong path to act as a guide and redirect them. Good old-fashioned love, concern, and hands-on support.

Therefore, you can best believe when you see the shift, that's usually the cause of wrong and bad influencers behind it. Parents, train yourselves to see and catch the switch-up or feel the energy. You all have been knowing your children most of their lives, but you have to know all the new people they have become to on and grew into as well.

Once you go on your kids' online accounts and space, you can see all of what they into and looking up. All their whole browsing history, too. One of the most effective tools and methods with your kids to get information and the truth out of them, whether they tell you directly or indirectly, is getting them to simply talk. When you engage and further question them or probing their online usage content, eventually they will crack and slip up and tell you the main answer to all your 20 different strategic questions. It will usually always be a noun. That's right, a person's name, a place or establishment, or a thing like a trend wave, a drug, or something new going around for them to indulge in.

When your daughter or son is begging to go over a certain friend or family member's house, maybe even an establishment that's usually their influence and seat of their new problem change and behavior switch. So usually all the wrong or bad influences in your kids' lives are always right under your nose and under their tongues. Just simply listen to the name they throw around all day or what they use as excuses at the foot of their problems, anger, and depression. Again, all kids feel like they are honestly one viral video away from being famous. This is the same fashion they pick up on or cling to social influencers, good, bad, or detrimental. Even with you using little hacks and tech methods of using certain apps to guard their content or even cutting off and controlling their WiFi, still is not as effective as you as an observant, engaged parent of prevention.

However, on the flip side of that, you can try and reverse engineer effect where you look for good influencers for them and suggest great influencers similar to your kids' liking and style. It's all framework that can stick if you present it right while you rebuild with your kids. This all while they are trying to figure out their true identity transitioning into adulthood. These kids nowadays are very smart and tech-savvy innovators, so you can simply tell them they can impact people or the world, they just have to create and work hard at carving out their own paths in life. Therefore, use all their favorite influencers as a structure design and template or simply motivation to be not like their favorite influencer, but better. Most of all themselves and the best version of self they can be.

Next we will go into the new social norms realm of today with the youth and proper prevention tools, tips, and structures. The new social norms all vary but are similar in pattern, similar to peer pressure, validation, trendy, and being very cool. The internet, school, or community can help encourage and enhance all social norms. It's the kids' or teens' choice to follow the way or wave path of the masses. Number one is popularity because everyone else is doing it in class or online, they, too, will follow and do.

Therefore, just as influencers, there are good social norms, bad social norms, crazy challenging social norms, and destructive social norms. Whereas, the parent must observe and evaluate which social norms to intervene and catch your kid or teens before they are inflicted or hurt themselves or hurt others indirectly following behind a destructive social norm, which is tons all over the world online in different societies. Some highly dangerous.

Remember you can catch all this by watching and feeling the kids or teens shift and mindset, including introverted kids, too. Adversity is the only way you grow thru it with your kids' journey into adulthood transition. We all have to go thru it.

The image kids hold of themselves or image they pick up from others and social norms is a based foundation which their entire personalities is made upon. Also this same image controls their behavior and circumstances. It's the new image they display to keep up with and stay in direct character of. You'll rarely see them out of character from the social norm image they are convinced to withhold, publicly and privately. Some kids do grow out of this stage. Others phase II this stage and further devote more time and cause to this imitated image from social norms and influencers they connected with. That same connection is an emotional attachment usually to fulfill a void of stress, acceptance, or past/hidden trauma. However, some parents refuse to accept this and reject it due to lack of energy, time-consuming, and always using a crutch, telling themselves their kid or teen is just going thru puberty or a growth period that will both change with time.

Which I highly disagreed with that method of approach, because this is the time of preventing and actualization to catch them before they fall or go further engaging down that dire destructive path, eventually enabling their development process structure. It's never too late.

Parents have great innate data and skills. Find good time to spend with them to help and save them by correcting their negative actions and wrong following. The main goal is to steer them back on their own righteous path to their own authentic self-discovery. Just like when they were babies and started to take the first baby steps, you would guard them so they did not hit their head, hurt themselves falling down, or walking into the wrong troubled areas. You must not be afraid, fatigued, or too busy to implement that same framework and using your natural parenting structural tools and agility. This is all part of evolving to the new ways of proper parenting prevention. The kids and teens are not babies no more. However, it is not wrong guarding them like a baby nowadays, especially if you see all this perpetual massive and school shootings as the new norms blasted across the media and internet. Kids copy that and suffering from depression and suicidal mental illness from the new social norms, influencers, and society pressures. It's pressure everywhere, in the home, schools, neighborhoods, groups, team, you name it for the kids. It's a lot and too much for them, that's why simple engagement and observation goes a long way.

The data shows a lot of the shooters carrying out the massive acts of violence always posted and stated before they wreak devastation aftermath of fatalities. Surprisingly, they were all ignored, neglected, and had fallen so far distanced in isolation that nobody stepped up to truly help them or did proper prevention tactics as parents, friends, or family. Even people who really suffer from mental illness. A lot of parents and people gave up or let go of their duty, being tired of dealing with inflicted issues and could simply do not know how to get their child help or even possibly too ashamed.

Do not worry. I wrote this book to connect, share, and engage with you parents. I am here to help you prevent and energy shift to help you continuously do right and help you be open to a new method of prevention. To work a different angle and tackle it with a victory and awareness one parent at a time. I love all y'all. Let's spread the word of prevention and save lives. All your works will bear fruit, not in vain, believe and feel that every day. Tell yourself it will be okay today and you got this, grab it by the handlebars and steer clear thru your parental navigation. Life is full of challenges and growth. Life is also good, especially if you really trust your innate process always.

If you think as parents it will not work, then no progress will formulate as any preventive tools and steps. Change and evolve the pillars of parenting to prevention. To equip you with the skills, tools, and mindset to help you achieve breakthrough, connection, awareness, engagement, and prevention with your kids.

Another prime example of social norms and influencers is an unfortunately sad story I want to share with you. It is a social norm now for teens to go to a random house and ring their doorbells and run away. Purely pranks for fun because all the kids are doing it and streaming it live on their feeds. The sad part of it is that 3 kids already lost their lives because of these same pranks across the nation. The latest kid rang the doorbell, took off running, the homeowner ran behind him chasing him, then eventually running the teen over with his car out of rage.

Apparently the homeowner stated this was the norm weekend pranks that he'd been suffering from prior to killing the last teen to do the social norm doorbell prank.

Now my question to you is, if these situations all have the proper preparation, awareness, accountability, could this have been prevented accordingly? You do not have to answer that question. Instead you can start with your children, watch their feed and content of their influences, social norms as prevention.

- Chapter 4 -

"The Warp of Perception"

To be proactive in prevention new actions and strategies, you must also need to understand the warp of perception, too. To make sure everyone truly knows the real meaning of perception, I'll define it for you to ensure we are on the same page and path going into this fourth chapter of the warp of perception.

Perception: An act or result of perceiving; awareness of one's environment through physical sensation; ability to understand, insight, comprehension.

Now let's put it into some context to be able to break down, do some framework, and problem solve with effective solutions and tips to help you further your new preventive skillset and tools.

The rapper Eminem's latest controversy single song and video. It's highly controversial because opposing views say

Eminem is making a mockery of the Las Vegas hotel shooter, reliving it, and projecting it in a glorified way with provoking lyrics, too.

However, Eminem's intention was to raise awareness to massive shootings, not to actually mimic them and to relive that awful day of sadness and loss of loved ones.

Therefore, this prime example is where exactly how the warp of perception attaches, acts, and shape-shifts kids' and teens' minds. His work of art as a prevention awareness method can actually backfire and a teen or kid can perceive it as translation being cool and the rapper is talking to them thru the music to act out, which ends up being a few random copycats acts of violence.

Even though Eminem does the lyrics and video from a troubled person's point of view, kids and teens can perceive it as the shooter's point of view, just the same as the adults did, too. This is how it warps perceptions and alters or bends a kid's or teen's mind frame going into adulthood.

Kids' or teens' minds usually do not distinguish between fact or fiction, reality or superimposed, imaginary and superficial, which is relating to the surface or appearance only. The reverse of this is to implement better content to help shape their own righteous and creative perception, which would lead them back down to a sure reality of certainty by further engagement and challenging their warp sense of perception, like their source and driven belief system that they are solely based on impulsive or altered decision making and poor judgement. Challenge their outsourcing and excuse system they narrate into their fragile egos. Kids' egos nowadays are super-sensitive, so they have to defend, lash out, or attach onto something or somebody, which they look for any perceptions to help feed, render, and protect the ego. Kids do not look at the ego as being their enemy or simply pride.

Another example of warp of perception is the social music app TikTok. Kids will say it's for girls only until they see boys their age dancing to the latest hit single and all the views plus their whole school participating in the challenge, too. All of a sudden the perception is changed and switched to acceptance and being okay and cool, which fires them up into activate go-mode. They disregard all prior perceptions, then attempt to go viral making their own personal videos for other boys and people to dance to with new steps and dance moves.

Therefore, society helps shape kids' perceptions. The pressure on kids today from social media and new norms alone is too much for them, especially with all this content that's extensive and highly competitive for their already short attention spans. The world evolving in tech and moving warp speed, advancing further by the minute. The kids get smothered into this and cannot reset or know how to drown out all the noise and stop the pull of the world. They deal with being judged 24/7 and under surveillance constantly by the weight of the world watching them. Nowadays it's a less more privacy. Kids cannot run and hide, retreat and vent. Instead they run and cry, they run from the parent and don't dare to share their problems or engage further with parents because they honestly believe the parents cannot relate and so out of touch with the reality of their world in real time.

Kids' level of intensity is tremendous. Instagram removes likes to take pressure off kids, too. Nowadays kids have to learn self-defense, violence, fear, and awareness at school for protection. A 10-year-old boy designed and patented a smart backpack with cameras to warn parents of bullying. Also for bully prevention. It was making news headlines online. The parents loved it and felt better to be aware of kids' well-being and safety. I also seen a company manufacturing kids' bulletproof backpack, too, for desperate measures and bully prevention measures. I believe the best alternative method of approach before all these protective mechanisms and tools starts within the home first from parent to child prevention proactively.

There are so many child monitoring apps like Bark that already help prevent 16 school shootings. It will also give you notifications of all your kids' online interactions, like keywords for cyber bullying, suicide, etc. Kids and teens cutting themselves and inflicting harm upon themselves in various ways struggle with clinical depression with perception warps that you as a parent cannot scope. You cannot simply scale back on your kids and teens. Support them, help them, and seek therapy or professional help. Mental health is more common than you would assume with all these distractions and trigger cue today for kids. Again, pulling them in each direction without enabling them to fully reset.

Parents, shift focus from judgement to love. Shift inner light, come more compassionate of social feed. You'd be amazed how deep love is and how much you can do to help change and challenge your kids' perceptions to positive actions, help, awareness of bullying, social acceptance, likes, selfies, and so on the list. Kids will adopt your policy sooner or later and be adaptive to their own.

Definition of bullying is imbalance of power over you. Hate driven. Don't let them have freedom of speech over you. Words only have power you give them, so do not give them power to warp and alter your perceptions.

Therefore, again, love is greater than hate. Love conquers all. Remember, you cannot fight fire with fire, it only fuels it. You also cannot fight mean with a mean. If you yell at people, they will show you the same yelling behavior right back. This is equally yoke to your kids, too, not just adults. Evil is organized and has a purpose to alter and perceive others under their havoc. Create an environment for you and your kids from love of what they like to engage in that's further them with success, peace, and enjoyment.

Do not let your kid be an independent child to perceive things freely and doing what they will/choose without no accountability or challenging them. Their identity thru osmosis goes up, behaving in a certain way and association. You need to help correctly alter their perception, identity, and consciousness.

Your personality is formed when you were a child. From the age of 1 to 5, we develop personal identity traits. Just like the infamous marshmallow test of kids' instant gratification where parents were advised not to feed their children breakfast that morning prior to the test. Then they challenge the kids with an offer of 2 marshmallows if they do not eat the one in front of them before the guy comes back in the room. The majority of the kids failed the test and either ate the whole marshmallow or ate a piece of it. See, this example is to show you if we already develop our personality, how easy it is to alter our perception once something is newly presented to us or move us to make a decision based solely on like, love, or a right that goes against prior perception base morality beliefs taught or innately. Kids and teens struggle with this 24/7 and cannot always make the best decisions. Parents cannot abandon this like a theory their kids have. Instead recognize and be aware to intervene proactively.

One of the largest warp perceptional phenomenons is gaming. A lot of people believed it's video games that cause kids to pick up guns and act out massive shootings because it warps their reality of perception to a fictitious reality from gaming world to real world. This superimposed augmented reality infused behavior is not to blame. However, we cannot ignore the underlying issue of the fact that gaming does have a dire effect on kids' perception and psyche. Certain shooting games and war games contribute to that perceptional warp, destroying some self-images higher than other gaming non-violence ones. Influenced easily by gaming, digital world, and social gaming with peers that can suffer an extremely warp of perception that affects your kids' and teens' mindset towards violence. Like it actually being okay to physically hurt somebody, shoot them, or even kill them.

Some kids and teens gaming is due to loneliness, bored, or peers. Parents cannot simply think that your kids are simply just gaming and cannot hurt nobody by gaming without being proactive and watch what games are they playing the most. Put timers on gaming, screen content. Your teens can hide gaming apps, games, pics, you name it, in different apps they download to hide things from parents, like the calculator or calendar that they think the parents are least to check or inspect. This how swift they are now so don't be afraid to check their data all around.

Next, interpretation is everything, and how you interpret your kids and how they interpret you is very important between feeling in the gaps. Possible rejection or miscommunication.

Take responsibility for interpretation and choose to see something, shift energy perception, joy to them, and attention. Simply by shifting one word, you can shift their perception and reality to create one from a righteous standpoint of view versus irrational or complex with devastation aftereffects.

Also, a reaction gives energy to things and entertain things. So please don't give in and play into your kids' wrong negative perceptions. That's badly influenced, which they will combat it and attempt to convince you it's highly logical and the new norms. When kids have a "have to" do things, they place it into a negative and as being forced to do.

Shifting key positive words help like being positive and encouraging energy with great accomplishment complements. You can simply reduce warp perceptions by rewarding them, liking and acknowledging positive perceptions. Let them be able to differentiate righteous. You just enable them back on path. Remember, explore more, have your kids over-explain, and exhaust them to get more details and the truth. Any incident or accident that triggered them, challenge them. It's different ways to connect and get a message across to kids simplify.

- Chapter 5 -

"Psychological Effects"

In this chapter of the psychological effect, it's crucial to tap into the youths' mind and the actualization of the aftereffect that takes a toll on them and control of them. Similar to a brainwashing inception that manifests into action and reality-based form.

The psychological effects all vary but plague all our youth with everything being exposed to them at their fingertips without parental discretion advisory. It's simply too accessible. Therefore, the psychological effects are highly common, spreading like wildfire rapidly.

This is also a strong suit we as parents have no ideal or simple solutions to fix or help our youth out of these trance-like effects and state of minds also. I will show you how to recognize the cause and effect that triggers and visual cues their sensory organs that release chemical in the brain to an action or feeling. This also affects what they think and speak. All negativity, profanity, bullying, suicidal, distress, and all toxic energy.

I also will discuss tips, methods, and the way the brain works to improve and replenish new psychological habit norms. Your kid or teen can rebuild and fix their psyche back into a healthy positive cognitive state. This is my aim and should be all parents' daily aim, making sure your child's mental space is healthy, happy, and clear to tackle one day at a time. It's true a healthy mind is a healthy, happy person. Everything a kid thinks on, does, emotions all initiate in the realm of their minds first.

Controlling your emotions helps make clear decisions. Depression, anger, frustration is all an emotion that starts within your mind. Kids numb themselves and further spiral plunge in addictions, ill behavior, substances, rage, etc. All from the psychological effect they are suffering from or simply bestowed upon them.

It's levels to consciousness. Your subconscious mind picks up things you allow to enter or what you perceive good or bad, right or wrong, reality or fiction. Then it replays it into your psyche until your consciousness spits it into an action or emotion, which leads to a feeling or you doing an actual act mind-based, craft to manifest into a sure reality. Some people use chants to guide them thru different dimensions altering consciousness. Others use tapping acute pressure points and other methods to alter their distress moods by changing the brain into an alpha state versus a beta state. Once your brain picks up on the signal, it alters mood and emotional state into different brain waves. This vibration or vibes and calm positive relax energy is a resetting tool and quick hack solution. However, the youth cannot pick up this sense and minds too underdeveloped to grasp it intellectually, especially with their peers' perceptions and influences. Plus they will think their parents' method is outdated or creepy for them to apply it in classrooms or public, being afraid to tap around people.

Even a meditation retreat to be clear and focused on self-esteem that reduces negative emotion, depression for a kid or teen is too hard and too much for their racing minds. The goal is an awakening and well-being state and emotional well-being, which is transformative psychological behavior. Emotion rage and outrage is common with the youth with all the distractions and triggers of the world. Therefore, non-applicable to them to relax, reset, and a meditation retreat like an adult can tune the world out to focus within. Undetected from your kids' conscious mind.

Next is the mental chatter, your inner dialogue or monologue. Same that goes on in kids' head makes it 10 times worse. Like mental models, a notion of this is the way the world works. Then kids get more evidence to prove what they think, but it's constructed by themselves.

Kids look for an escape and fast-fix relief. Kids scroll all day and it feeds ego in certain things further, likes, and appeal to them. It triggers their brain. The past impacts your psyche and how it's built, like a transpersonal dimension. They suppress different things. For instance, low self-esteem, fear, shame, feeling suicidal, and depression. However, to a resolution being able to see yourself different and better every day helps. How to shift from one level to the next level of consciousness. Let go of the emotion and the cause or addiction is gone. You must try to impact and instill in your kids' head daily. It triggers their brain to help stimulate and them see, feel, and do better. Remember the goal is to be proactive parents, not reactive to kids and things.

Kids' psyche for survival is challenging growing up. A culture where young, beauty, popularity, and money-driven.

Advertising negative or positive self-images of ideal body shaming and appearance has psychological effects to their egos. They are more seeking reacting from people and the culture, not their actual parents and family.

Kids and teens look for comfort and convenience. Kids will open up more and talk to their parents more than one-word answers. Like if you ask, how was school today? And they answer, good, or okay, maybe even fine is all one-word reply versus real trust and engagement with longer dialogue or even monologue if they feeling good in that space.

When they feel you're their friend and you use a befriend approach angle, they will let their guards down and feel safe and comfortable, like they can relate to you like their friend at school they engage with being themselves around, or what they have grown into new self and space. It may be awkward at first, but live in the present with them, no coasting or zombified to the phone glued. It's about time and quality experience being determined daily. Kids are very observant and notice and feel all if you being truly sincere and committed to their best interest at heart and well-being.

The parents and kids phase has really done changed. Social digital platforms are driven as world means, especially with kids and teens spending average of 2 years of their lives online. This shows you it's definitely time for awakening and proper prevention. Understanding your kids' psychological effects is another element to digest and help you assess your developmental counter proactive skills with a detailed process plan implemented. Kids develop this psychosis thru their distress environments, online, or drugs. Furthering mental health illness and driving it to an unsafe place to hurt themselves or others.

Let's tap back into the brain further how it works and its dynamic structures and senses. The mind switch, trigger a switch in your central nervous system. Like calm and collect, rest and digest stage also alter moods, too.

Neurons are cells in your brain. Neurogenesis makes new brain cells/neurons. Synapse connect between 2 neurons. Activity like workouts, reading, etc., with positive results help build new brain cells. Improvement and adaptation is a must to help build your synapse strong, sound, and image of the brain. Remember neurons that fire together wire together. Also learning in plasticity, ways the brain can change and develop, and grow all ages.

Brain also produces chemical releases with electric signals, like dopamine, glutamate, and serotonin, which alters or enhances your senses, moods of stimulation, and reward-based system of instant gratification and so on. 10 percent of serotonin is produced in your gut that makes you feel good or crave response.

The brain is pulsing with chemical and electric pulses and waves, electric connections from frontal lobe to your left and right brain and all your central nervous system. Kids have hundreds and trillions of connections, way more than adults. The brain is a massive engineer and mastery of developments and learning languages. Within 3 years the child talks, walks, and brain wired to learn at a rapid pace.

Speaking, listening, and understanding kids pick up extremely well. You can shape your own brain with every syllable and sound kids do. The human brain is highly adaptable to anything possible. The system of neurons in the brains master skills of language, the vowels and consonants that make up words and building blocks.

Thought waves, what we think about we process, therefore we need to change our thought process and stress thoughts that alter our moods and behavior. This is how instead of helping kids to transition, you deny them and disengagement leads to further disassemble to enable their transition phase troubleshoot areas, stunting their growth and focal points good and bad. They need to be wealthy in emotional terms, too. It all leads to cognitive healthy space and mental health.

Create new tools to help shape their psychological effects. Their happiness will never last if you have expectations on it because they will fail, feeling forced to impress and uphold into your parenting mode that you see them as versus what they see themselves as or developing to their authentic versions of self.

Test and learn. Crafting experience, testing new areas and methods. Socializing performances, small things and approaching parenting in a different form, then find out how kids respond to new ways. Then you will see what works, hurts, or help bring them to their corrective path of life.

Work out what your differences are, and develop and adapt to change to new environment. Turn your responses into questions, helps to formulate a new investigation to probe your child more for the truth, problem, and reasons. Then you'll be revealed into what areas to fix and what is the cause of the breakage. A lot of kids and teens feel broken, unaccepted, or looking for a place to belong. This all aligns with their psychological effect and footprint of themselves.

Further, try to look for patterns, change of behaviors, identify patterns common or emotions and values that cause of it. If you lose your connect time with children or your rhythm, you must find a new one. Go deeper than the surface approach and standard norm.

Our brain is founded on pattern of trust. Find ways to further advance and engage in your brain. To become a thinker of common solutions in ways that only you been knowing your own child since day 1. Not the world of school and social media, but your own framework intimacy with your child. Remember that you must engage brain to adapt with kids further is your main focus starting point.

It always starts with one step and one day at a time to implement any new system and process. You just have to get kids in new choices, new spots, places, and space. New environment change is a proven study experience. A new environment, people, and socialization will all help change the abnormal psychological effects kids suffer from.

- Chapter 6 -

"Patterns & Behavior Changes"

This chapter is key to detect mental health illness at scope before it gets worse. Also looking for the signs, paying attention to kids' actions, moods, patterns, and all behavior changes. This is not just exclusive to mental health awareness, but any patterns and behavior changes awareness of your kids and teens. I'll show you how to recognize it, counter it, and solution to fix it and help them thru yet another transitional phase of their lives before adulthood or it's too late.

The ideal model approaching old systems in new ways, to learn spotting behavior changes, design intervention, self-awareness, and pattern recognition. Also including emotion recognition, mood management, stress management, and neural stimulations and triggers.

If your kid is having a bad day at school, being bullied, or can't focus and dealing with depression, it's usually an action or mood attached. Distress leads to mood changing or inferiority. Acceptance and peer or social validation can lead to them lashing out, cussing, or just simply anything attention-seeking to be seen in anyway, by any person or platform. Also your kid being abused verbally, physically, or mentally can lead to them feeling hurt, suicidal, or life inflicting pain on others or themselves like cutting themselves or other pain tolerance inducements. If your kid is being bullied, they can also transform that hurtful pain into negative energy and feed off or bully other people, family, and friends that's more vulnerable at state. This is where you see the older sibling pick on and bully the younger sibling or neighbor's younger child.

The kids and teens cannot transform these behavior changes into positive channels like telling people stick and stones will break my bones and words will never hurt me. They cannot relate their hurt and pain with parents, adults, or other peers. Instead they go with it versus against it. Fighting fire with fire and giving the reason a reaction by giving definition and acknowledging the problem giving life, power to alter their moods, behaviors, and patterns of negativity. These all affect kids' ability to connect. This is where you step in, intervene, follow the patterns, read between the lines, see their distress or troubled behavior. Remember kids or teens will hardly ever talk to you about their current ongoing situation or conditions sincerely with the truth. That's the reality of today with actualization of kids masking their hurt, pain, and distress in this rude with a biting attitude world. It's a popularity, social validation, fame-seeking, and chosen society pressure of norms.

Kids truly want to connect by the heart to origin and want to be anonymous because they undervalued. Kids also feel their value is in base of things material driven. They want common ground and value.

You have to learn how to connect, learn how to understand their patterns and behavior changes first to help them or others. They ask, am I accepted, loved, where do I belong, and life purpose? Kids are searching for reason and purpose everywhere and picking up on everything like they did as babies.

Be a bridge to them while they are developing and going thru these patterns and behavior changes suddenly. Don't let your kids be your blind spot. You cannot be dismissive of kids' feelings or isolated and secluded, shutting off and not allowing them to get too close to you.

Kids suffer with guilt leads to shame. Once you know you're loved, your value, strength, awareness all increase. We all are broken somewhere and looking to be fixed. You need to know you loved as you are, to do better and find your potential.

Dialogue and relating to your kids of what exact battle they getting thru. You need to dig and shape it, shift it, drive it, and define it in scope. Expect to have a toolkit. Let them see they have a purpose behind their pain and a way how to deflect it, and a way to dig deeper to overcome it, versus dwelling on it and emotional state.

Meta cognition, change/trick your brain. You interpret pattern loops, your gear box, it moves and awakens affect in your frontal cortex to change and learn new things. Triggers a new moment to change and prompts you to move. Just like 5-second rule, interpret patterns, and autopilot to act. Then to start new habits and behaviors.

We all have patterns and watch people patterns. The main loophole in pattern and behavior modification is focus. Like a focus on what you have or what's missing. What you're missing hurts. A focus on what you can or cannot control, or a focus on past, present, future. A pattern of focusing on what's missing, can't, and past.

You need to take control with kids and have them focus on positive likable things for them that challenges them in a comfortable non-pressure way. Also a choice to help kids better wave and vibration going in fresh level head versus stress, angry, or depression that complex pressure and triggers them. Do not focus on meeting needs with expectation barriers. Focus on adding value with your kids and others the ability to add real value to allow disengage with wrong patterns and behavior to make proficient choices for the good patterns, behaviors, and pressure. Develop skills and ability to enable them and switch their direct focus. Motive matters, growing, learning, and giving feels 10 times better.

No thinking bias or cognitive bias in your parenting intervention and prevention on the hook of these pattern loops and behavior changes. Have a real impact on your kids for them to feel safe in shaping their own health patterns and behavior.

Actively listen, check their development skills communication in sets of behaviors. Look for buzzwords. Reflect on own strengths. Assess level of kids' areas needs to develop. Again, kids won't accept parents' past because they simply want to push their own future. People are connected like never before.

Kids are tapped in, breaking down barriers thru platforms and patterns. Whereas, those same shared values kids and teens have, parents need to build resilience in their kids, too. Not just from their online shared community popular loop patterns and behaviors.

Next is shifting connections. Look at how you recognize patterns and behavior, then how you interact with your kids and evolve, grow, change, and learn. You must see your kids or parenting in a different or new way. Even social activities and different conversations with kids and experiences, too.

Look back and say, what do kids actually mean? Then build communication, values of reflecting and habit as an exercise. Try something new, a new approach and aspect from kids. Get feedback from them and take initiative plan into action.

It's a whole wide new network to tap into, learn, and evolve. Support groups, master classes, parenting awareness programs all online. Do new framework of teaching and learn new habits of kids. Develop psychiatric tools. I know your values and experiences change over time. Don't evaluate your own, because even if your household is in check, things can still happen suddenly and drastically. No one's exempt from proper preparation of prevention. It's just like the same concept of driving a car without a seatbelt because you're an expert driver or a safety driver, it still doesn't protect you if you get into a car accident like if you simply took the initiative to buckle up.

You can also do a reverse engineering process to problem solve these patterns and erratic behavior changes by pattern interruptions. Simply do pattern interruption by disrupting their patterns, surroundings, and environment. It's just same method like disrupting the status quo. Distract them from their distractions and disruptive patterns and behavior. It is a lot of schools of thoughts, methods, but you must evolve your old rules of thumb. Application is constantly applying new and effective ways to break through and connect to your kids and teens during these patterns and behavior changes before they perpetual lapse and permeate into alter ego of devastation into adulthood and the real world outside of home life.

Finally, let's jump back into the mental health topic. Some believe this subject is too messy because it's hard to deal with and it advances before you can get them treatment. A lot of people don't want to take the time out with people struggling with mental health disease or suffering from bipolar-manic depression, paranoia, and psychopathic, or even schizophrenia traits, symptoms, or patterns and behavior changes of psychosis, period.

However, mental health is the number one blame on massive shootings and school shootings in the U.S. data that we cannot seem to get a handle on or a direct effective solution process. It's beyond an evaluation or prescribed psych meds. That's because most parents, coworkers, teachers, and students are unaware and cannot see the signs or read between the lines before the person suffering lashes out in that devastating fatal rage act of violence, taking multiple victims and families down with them. Therefore, once someone explodes into these brazen assault acts, everyone that knew the individual automatically says they lost their mind, they do not know what got into that person, or that person is normal, a good and kind introvert person. When in all actuality, that same individual has been suffering mental illness, mind been slipping or changing right before your eyes. People ignore or neglect to see and deal with the signs of pattern and behavior changes.

This is the main pillar I based this book to handwrite with prevent to make sure we all responsible to hold our own kids accountable in the home first and the neighbors or classmates if you are aware. Then spread parent-to-parent, start online communities of prevention to be proactive to massive shootings beforehand to help stop them by getting your kids proper help, evaluation, mentors, programs, activities, events, and even the proper meds if that's extremely needed also.

Parents, be understanding and highly competent of mental health traits and awareness. Like you may think your kid is timid and a late bloomer to spread their wings, when really it can be paranoia, which is a psychosis, too, marked by delusions and irrational suspicion usually without hallucinations. Psychosis is a serious mental illness like schizophrenia marked by loss of or greatly lessened ability to test whether what one is thinking and feeling about the real world is really true. Psychosocial is involving both, psychological and social aspects. Relating social conditions to mental health.

Therefore, it is so important to get help for your kids and teens in this vast space and common in one out of every 6 teens. It's never too late to educate and engage with mental health.

- Chapter 7 -

"Engagement"

Having a deep connection with your kids is an element to engagement. Like really actualize and dig deeper than the surface with kids. Seeing all the signs, traits, and feeling the energy. Being proactive, reactive, and problem solving to further engage and establish better relationships and trust. It's therapy to be well engaged with them, besides the template of child engagement you have set from previous generations that you adopted as a route to instill in them, too, which nowadays is the old traditional way of child engagement that most kids are sick of and will tell you it's too old, boring, and they need way more time and attention or simply your help during all their transcending stages into teen and adulthood.

There are different rules and types of engagement I will go over with you in this chapter as well. Most parents are not aware how to perpetuate engagement and energy interactively with their kids and teens at home or with schooling. I will help you push your engagement meter to the max to enable you on your proper prevention path and accountability.

Disengagement is first, which is the underlying issue that majority of the households suffer from. They are disengaged and unattached genuinely and attentively, like being too busy and only pay for your kids' school tangibles, going to events, present but not literally present in the moment of engagement and validation your kids seek. They look for signs and read your obvious face and body language to see you're not fully engaged or paying them no true attention like other classmates' excited parents. You cannot simply give your kids a tablet or game console and latest games expecting that as doing your job and standard engagement. If so, you are wrong and this is a huge disengagement. Another way is work life versus saving your kids and other lives. This is where you're fully engaged in work life, not fully engaged in your home life. Or some parents are not fully engaged in themselves, so they do not know how to be fully engaged with nobody else, being unable to reset, reassess, and what next step to take to further engage with a new approach.

This is all disengagement. You can service others, but not self and family, or take time off and an actual engagement class, even listening to an Audible, to help you advance versus disengagement. Disengagement is like a detrimental effect that snowballs on your family, kids, and environment. Same way if you disengage at work, you're most likely to be fired in real time. I also know that some people believe engagement is fundamental. However, majority parents cannot process it in new fundamental ways of growth with your kids' innate and physical growth simultaneously.

Now we will go over all types of engagement: good, bad, healthy, joyful, etc. You can also over-engage and being intrusive and inverted. First let's define engage—to connect or interlock, mesh, and commence. Or to cause to take part and participate. Thru the initial stage of engaging, a smile, facial expressions, and body language have to be positive to set your demeanor with your kids. Engagement is not always hostile like you are in a war, engaging in mortal combat with your kids. Engagement is all the appointments you make and set with your kids. It's also employment and your job as a parent to perpetuate in new active ideal ways.

Positive engaging is being proactive by encouraging your kids' confidence with a manner of positive body language, tone, eye contact, and assurance. If your kids see this, it will establish a safety net if they fall short of their aim. However, if you are positive in every attribute of building their confidence, they will succeed because of the trust they feel is there of surety.

Good engaging is being counterproductive to keep asking your kids questions to make them see you are truly concerned and their day and stories matter. They will let their guards down and feel more comfortable around you and opening up with you, especially if you a girl-dad. Good engaging is very therapeutic for kids and teens, next will be moved over into the parent/friend category where they will open more and be actively engaged with you sparking the conversations and initiating interactions.

This good engaging is where every parent first started off at one point, that gradually lost its value in the course of the kids' and teens' growth process or the influence by the culture, class, and online.

We lose this good engaging and it leads to bad engaging. Therefore all your prior engagement becomes toxic because you cannot break down the kids' and teens' barriers. Your next step is to force entry and breach their barriers, violating their personal and mental space, which is reverse way to regain that good engaging and trust. They literally will despise being physically around you and at home. They retreat to a safe place, room, and to their edevices and gaming consoles. They can actually build toxic brain patterns to behave in a bizarre way. Design a system.

Healthy engaging is taking your kids out of stressful or toxic environments where they can interact in a visual, mental, and physical stimulation. It's about creating new or better experiences to connect with them that bring peace, joy, and inner happiness. Even if it's taking them out to their favorite place to eat, relax, and engage. Most healthy engaging is about timeout and space. Clear space helps the engagement organically grow versus total reactive and response engaging.

Life is to follow a passion or path in this journey on Earth for kids and adults. Try to experience every emotion, gift, and growth engaging. However, don't bestow your premise on others to will your fulfillment.

You must develop a new system with engaging as a parent of active prevention. However, do not increase narcissism in your kids. You cannot train for confidence. It's not connected to a skill level. It has to be a reward after it's done. You gain confidence after each little accomplishment in a kid.

Tackle what most are afraid of, then embrace your new process of engaging and innate balance in your kids' lives. We all have the capacity to transfer energy to each other. Confrontation, to confront with your kids having the convo, telling the truth. Do it tangible. Be willing to confront your kids, problems, and tell the truth. In all areas, progress, schooling, so expand comfort zone. Challenge yourself.

Framework of good engaging is creative tools you use to structure and implement, like asking kids what they learned. Key asking questions what they learned to tie into real life. Once they see your eyes light up and you engaged into what they doing or what their game is about they playing. How to adjust, focus, and learn. What they learn can apply to life or sport, etc. That's the challenge. Nowadays kids can get egames scholarships, so there is a positive engaging narrative there to be made and reversed of them playing all day. Instead switch their gaming content and limited hours. Then, tell them the more rewarding games of prizes, scholarship, and what they can make a career of or maybe even programming video games. You would be surprised how well they will respond actively and see increased positive engaging in the home.

It's like kids living in two different worlds, from social platforms, then real life versus online, your IRL life, especially in crossover dealing with crossroads in life. Also sitting from people for direct eye contact engagement is better to connect with kids versus across room or sideways.

Next, integrity is being whole with one and all, your word, etc. Must keep it so kids see and look as you being an example of ideal or model integrity. When you break your word and self-worth goes down, then over time, your creditability goes down, too. Kids don't believe in your power of words or you. So parents, you must declare and deliver on it. Integrity helps hold kids accountable.

If you expect more, you get more. If you expect less, you get less, too. This is the same model in prevention parenting. Please be steadfast, don't have a breakdown, have a breakthrough with your children. Use enthusiasm, power, and passion to connect and engage with your kids to move them. It's a choice to feel it and them feel it, too. Even if it's an intense process. Your enthusiasm is a choice, love is a choice, joy is a choice. If you not fired up with enthusiasm, you'll be fired by enthusiasm. If you not all in with your kids' lives, you all out. All means your enthusiasms.

Step your kids up in a positive engaging way to impact, inspire, and coach them. Help implement your kids' journey into the pursuit of happiness, physical, mental, maturity to once you have your system in line with kids, and you implement it or alter it, keep at it, and refine it, repeat it and continue to grow. Transpire them with new system and in their transitional phase.

Competence they feeling and being capable to engage clearly and relatedness. If your kids or teens seem disorientated, it can be signs of drug abuse or mental illness. This is where you more likely to attempt different trials of engaging methods to further regard their responses and impulses. Also autonomy personal control and initiative. If you cannot make choice of what you do, how your engagement match your kids' value and the reinforcement of your flexibility, dedication to cause, have a balance between working role and other roles in your life, use a structured creative process. Write pros and cons list to help which prioritize engagements, values, and decision making that's important to you. Then categorizing critical, important, desirable, optional engaging goals. Forced choices, pairs, if you had to choose, which engagement values win the most bouts, uncognitive and cognitive demeanor.

Progressive elimination, which would you use, then the first one you would drop. These are three methods you can use to identify engagement value. Ranging most have black and white, thus recognize when life role, balance, and interact with kids, teens, and people or events. Look for maximum range when you look for engagement value. The max and minimum of your range until you have it down pat what you wrote on paper to implement your newfound system of perpetuating your engaging with your kids, teens and household. Remember the three core features, too. Authenticity/energy, balance, and challenge. Draw your own pie chart to challenge yourself, corrective balance between workplace, home life, personal time, and engagement. Lastly, your positive energy prior to going into engaging with your kids, that energy is highly effective, like a swing vote that gives life to positive engaging with positive actions and moods from your kids' and teens' interaction proactively.

Parents, commit to something, focus, and take action as a preventive cautionary measure as a pro tool. Whatever you focus on, you'll feel and achieve it with a natural innate parental instinct of problem solving. However, work and determination is tackling your fear and those question marks of what to do.

- Chapter 8 -

"Awareness"

Awareness is having perception or knowledge, conscious, or informed. Vigil is to watch. Vigilant is being alertly watchful especially to avoid danger. Agile is to be able to move quickly and easily. Observant is watchful, keen, perceptive, mindful. Lastly, observation is designed for use in viewing, or in making solid observations. The gathering of information by noting facts or occurrences and a conclusion drawn from observing.

Then you have scope, which is space or opportunity for action or thought. Extent covered, range, also an instrument for viewing. Dissatisfied kids are caused by parents not of scope.

Now that you understood that you can understand awareness and the law of active awareness perpetual duty. Awareness is like the Energizer bunny, it keeps going and going. Awareness is a full job in scope that you must have energy for. It's not time putting in, it's definitely an energy force to actively take action of awareness of kids and surrounding environments daily. It's not a task or statement, it should be a way of life as a parent of prevention.

The pivot of awareness is to never get too lapsed in your overview of things your ego makes excuses for and dumb down to allow to ignore red-flag signs and kicking your feet up in dismissal. You cannot have disregard of your conscious mind and clear signs. The story you tell yourself in a first-person perspective versus someone else's point of view blinds your awareness and alters the plot, sequences, and outcome. This is where the conflict occurs from within the parents' and kids' lineage turmoil breakage of connections thru awareness. Thus, creates generational gaps, which is hard for kids and teens of this at-your-fingertips era with everything being placed in front of them versus textbook learning hands-on the old traditional ways. So you need to be aware of all the components within their boundaries and the scope of your own as a parent.

Let's put this into a clear context to grasp better. Remember this, the way we are aware of our lives is how we shape it.

Therefore, change your awareness to change your life and loved ones' life, too.

As Kobe Bryant once stated, it's not the destination, it's the journey of awareness. The aim and scope of awareness. Relax, spend time on self, turn off the phone, and get back grounded to your natural self, then recharge with deep breaths of positive energy. To be aware of the universe, you must take in the universe to breathe in and see it for what you are not normally trained to see. A leader finds ways to get people to believe in you and themselves awareness and agile.

There are plenty of things as parents we are unaware of that we lack in our natural awareness periphery. This is how kids mastermind things right under the parents' nose. Some in actual plain sight, too. The average observant skill is shot to hell because of the new norm of process overload. Between work life, parenting, technology, financial, and distress of long hours, no sleep.

Ask yourself, what is your kids' hidden agendas? How to discover it, bring it out or alter it? The answer and first solution is awareness. Certain addictions consume them, like gaming, scrolling online, binge watching, even possibly being a bully. The key is to be aware of all their transitional cues.

All the signs will be there if you are actively alert and you set up a natural parenting alert system. However, first you must throw out the old alert system and innovate accordingly as the time prevails new distractions, influences, and social norms of predatory behavior. Be careful of kids' company online that they're not getting recruited or influenced. Without fully awareness, your kids are already easily influenced. I have seen a 3-year-old on the TikTok app dancing. Even though it was all fun and games, it just shows you the power of influence and social-influenced frenzy that can move or take your kids under the influence, too. Provocative, aggressive, enticed, or derogatory influences. However, you can be proactive and catch with due awareness.

Not wanting to change who you are, what you are, or what you do will only hurt yourself, kids, and household. It cannot be wholeness in one way without contradictions. It's a time and place for everything. Having boundaries and getting up to take action for awareness to change before it's a tipping point in your life or an explosive way with your kids. Even if you worn down and so exhausted, don't give up, let go, or stop your mission of betterment. You don't need more outputs and outsourcing to help you as a dealing tool to cope day-to-day. With your intuition, you trust it, act on it, and create space and tools that save you money. You'll be able to look back and view a better situation. A lot of parents want to avoid it and new system and cannot clear out their minds, schedules, and turn off their phones. In that fogginess in your mind that you have been dealing with for years or decades, you cannot clear because the process you cannot figure out past burnout. Contemplating the process you have in your head on how to find new routes to awareness, methods, and practices. Your thought process has to be clear, challenging, and realistic with yourself to become a better human being. If you are not broken in your thought process, work, or home, that does not mean your kids' process is not broken. So you strive for some space and solutions start to come in. It makes you have compassion to people and awareness just taking the initiative. Being aware is easy, implementation to awareness is hard. Being disconnected from awareness of your kids, surroundings, and drive to serve and protect, is fear of insight. We want to believe the reward and payoff of our kids if we as parents do as right to our duty. Have a 360-degree view and discerning. You may feel like you are not getting ahead, but your decisions will be clear and stage at your kitchen table, broadcasting to your family being assertive in all their awareness. Like their schedule, grades, hangouts, and daily progress, which fuels aspiration and clarity in their lives, what's right and what's wrong. You may not have to implement a plan of awareness, just have that desire and relate. Accountability is awareness, too. You can move forward and progress within, especially what are you watching and aware of daily in your environment.

To raise awareness in others and parents, you have to first have a systematically intervention. It's no discerning without awareness, and there can be no true intervention without being in total awareness, too. Intervention is another source of awareness that each parent can be proactive with, especially spreading awareness in the community, schools, or online groups, too. Awareness is to keeping parental focus on kids' and teens' choice, behavior, mental space, and associations.

The number-one problem is your kids' actions and what they have become and bad habits they developed under your household directly or indirectly. The effect is kids bullying other kids, developing drug abuse, or acting out of pure impulse of devastating actions caused, which usually ends in rage, mental illness, and random acts of violence. Next is the framework and practical tools for effective solution for awareness in scope for your proper prevention, new implementation challenge to save your kids' lives and others. Most people get motivated, then get right back lazy a few days later, distrust of their own system implementation process. Also your kid can be so relentless to your new accountability and observability that you give up and let go because it's too confrontational and too much of a headache for you to perpetuate. You must stick to your guns as a parent or do not be too afraid to reach out to get help. It can be to other family members, coaches, mentors, even psychiatrist.

It's never too late. It's all about your committed devotion to your awareness prevention. Remember every single person after a tragedy or a massive shooting first response to their child acts of violence or suicide, they state that they were totally unaware. Unaware of their child's mental illness, erratic behavior changes, engagements, or their prior associations and wrong influences. Even being a copycat act of violence and cyber-recruited, all the parents claim no idea or no trace of insight, being totally in the blind and most of all unaware. The next thing every other parent says in denial is not my kid because they would not dare, or they say they as parents are too attentive to their kids. Well, not according to the data. Our social society violence is increasing yearly, especially in school and massive shooting. Bullying is more on the rise, you just don't hear it making headlines as much as the tragedies, but it's still there relevant. Therefore, some of the kids must be slipping thru the cracks right under the parents' nose in the household. Guard their computer, edevices, affiliation, and time of place. It's all relevant in true proactive awareness to keep one upper hand on your kids and true accountability.

Take 100 percent responsibility for kids and people in your life. No excuses. You cannot control your kids' actions, but see and be aware of your part in it. Your actions have to contribute to others, including your kids and household. Please don't depreciate your value in kids and appreciate work, social life, and happiness when you're actually depreciating.

Understand the psychology behind it, the science behind it, define our meaning of what happens that don't serve us. We get into autopilot ways again, lacking our vigilant capabilities. The hardship you been thru with your kids and growth process, but it's that deep connection and purpose. The contribution, love, and message you want to send and the tone of environment you want in your life and surroundings. Freedom, love, success, and health versus destruction, darkness, and evil from not being hands-on observant with fully devoted awareness no matter how mentally or physically exhausted you are as a parent. Your kids, teens, and household will thank you later, most definitely. Maybe your neighbor or community will thank you, too, someday.

Awareness is the key and the most important asset. The parents are the authority, period, to evaluate and reinforce. It's always about decision making and all parents have a choice from doing a good job or a great job versus autopilot decision making like Google does with decision making process and algorithm reply answers. It's parental pressure to stay steadfast in their conquest process of awareness.

The way we narrate our lives is how we shape it, so we change our narrative to change our life and ways or habits. You must edit your story, look at positive things and people in your story around you. In order to be a wise editor, we need to be realistic and truthful to others and ourselves. People are not willing to see their point of view as a narrator. If we can get out of first character and be aware by looking at it from other person's point of view, the story becomes vivid and opens up in the context and interest. We distort all our stories and alternative narratives. So don't reject your plan of entry on new awareness tools you suggest the strategy for kids and household structure.

- Chapter 9 -

"Triggers"

In this chapter on triggers we will show all the triggers and how they act as a set-off mechanism. It's the last stand or straw that snapped and caused them to go off and all-out. This includes suicide and overt acts of terror and violence. You cannot really train or prepare for triggers because usually it's too late once they get to that breaking boiling point of being upset to where it manifests outwards into affirmative actions of conflict, turmoil, or devastation.

Even though with engaging you can see the cause and root of some of your child's triggers, you cannot stop all their triggers. Especially the sensitive hair-trigger ones. However, you can counter them and be counteractive with another reverse engineer approach, too. This is not easy and very challenging, but once you catch them as they manifest, you can probe and ask more questions, like what set them off.

The cause and effect? Then why is their outcome a negative or impulse reaction? Which can stem from a number of things. Emotional, irritated, buzzwords, music, fear, or incompetence.

Now let's tackle triggers, the cause and effect, and different types, before you can come up with a precise power tool to avoid these triggers until your kids grow out of them or learn how to self-manage them like most adults. The key is to ultimately avoid triggers and have a framework processing to deal with them accordingly. Don't let kids outsmart you, avoid you, bribe you, trick you, or deceive you, too. Kids and teens have govern on their life, you must alter and enhance that govern or thermostat.

First I will define trigger. A trigger means to activate, to initiate, or set off as if by a trigger like a verbal remark, etc. Actuate means to put into action or to move to action.

You have emotional triggers, visual triggers, mental triggers, environmental triggers, influential triggers, music triggers, energy triggers, mood triggers like happy or sad triggers, and so on. These are the main focal triggers with kids and teens. It's also adult triggers, too. For example, passion, trust, alarm, rebellion, and mystique left-brain seeking prestige being likable. The most popular adult trigger is shaming, especially with all the tech-savvy social platform. Fat shaming or shade triggers all comes from within self, but comes out as an obscene bully type, a personality of aggressive and passing judgements. For example, a shame trigger for men is do not believe to be weak or perceived weak. So vulnerability is looked at as soft and triggers the men egos, which in reality is a social pressure trigger, caused by society and social norms. Whereas, an example of a woman shame trigger, on the other hand, is to not sweat, and make it look effortless and perfect while still being hot. Stay hot and awesome 24/7 and pious as a woman. Therefore, it's society categories that people classify you or themselves under, causing social pressure triggers, too.

Now with your kids and teens, you have to know what are their ticking points to where it triggers them to go off like a bomb. That explosive friction, conflict, or reaction. Do you watch your kids and notice how video games, social media, music, or certain subjects trigger them off like a rocket ship? Maybe it's fear, being very inferior of certain aspects and challenges from life, school, or peers. The toxic environment is the cause and effect that catapults and leads to a trigger reaction. Some kids, teens, or people triggers are more easily triggered or tolerant than others. It may be driven or infused and influence to spiral out of control. Also the snowball theorem is placed effectively accordingly to how triggers snowball gradually and increase with rapid flow, building up to where it's too heavy and manageable and become out of control, crash and splat all over the place. This is a parent's or anybody's worst nightmare is a deadly trigger of eruption and evil lured aggression typical ensue violence or triggers suicidal tendency. Of course that is an emotional and mental health trigger. Some triggers are like earthquakes, most get blindsided or simply don't see it coming.

You can counter triggers after you take true notice and see what triggers them, the same way you do with your spouse or friends, then you can evaluate how to prevent them from running into those same trigger traps. Avoidance at scope is the first stage and mission goal. Here is how it works and processes in the mind. The distress brainflow from a cognitive beta wave to an alpha brainwave to alter your troubling distress or emotional mood. It's four stages how your brain processes it. First is the struggle stage, the release stage, the flow stage, and finally the recovery state. Therefore, from the problematic chaos you can either create the change and avoid or don't fuel the trigger, or are you going to create the chaos and perpetuate fueling your triggers to manifestation.

We must provide alternate solutions to help kids and teens simplify their means of chaos getting a little awkward to create ways or templates to destroy chaotic triggers. Distractions cue triggers with kids and teens. Therefore, distractions are the number-one enemy trigger. They get annoyed and upset or highly irritated from the world distractions. Opposing forces or equilibrium is balance. 98 percent of transformation is body and environment.

Cue triggers and visual cue triggers most kids and teens suffer from. Even though some triggers are a growing transitional stage from adolescent, teen, and adulthood, more adults take triggers from their childhood, especially the fearful triggers. Like the self-doubt, lack of confidence, and self-sabotaging of inferior triggers. All the wide range of hardship and emotion they try to decipher and cannot process them leads to all trigger response and reactions. It drives their mental and they become overwhelmed, blinded, or lost. A visual cue trigger can be simple as a certain item they see to set them off. Or a person that the child had a bad experience with. A more prominent visual cue trigger for them is like seeing a person that inflicted trauma, abuse, or overwhelmed them emotionally. This ignites into an explosive trigger of hurt, where they immediately lash out from their protective space. Similar to the fight-or-flight human adult response nature.

Most kids do not have that instinct developed to assess and deal with each crisis situation. Therefore, their natural instinct is to pull a trigger of outrage and act up by lashing out, some even screaming and yelling profanity, or even throwing objects and damaging property. Some kids' triggers may even go as far as threatening others, themselves, and cutting themselves or burning themselves. This visual cue trigger works the similar way with adults. For example, if you see an ex, you get enraged or emotional. Either way there is a response and an immediate reaction. Adults may keep it all inside without acting out, causing a scene, or bringing attention to yourself. Most because you have embraced your triggers and imbalanced them. Maybe you really don't want to give your ex the benefit of the doubt and see them trigger you. Now the question is after your recent split or break-up with your ex, and you see them with someone else online or in a public place, does that trigger you in a reactive way or innate trigger reflex?

With these examples it may be a lot more easier to deal with as an adult dealing with triggers and managing them thru ultimate of years of experiences, good or bad. This is not so the case with kids, they are unaware and undeveloped. This is where you as parents are very aware of all their triggers, then help your kids to identify their triggers after each episode and show them how to properly respond and deal with them formal. It's practical and you simply cannot give your kids an inch of space and leave them to deal with the aftermath because they are upset or throwing you the secluded silent treatment. They will cope if you give the true proper tools to transition. Like asking them look at what was the cause, then seeing the effect. Next giving them ways they can go around that trigger, preventing the episode or simply remove themselves from certain triggers. However, the end goal is to get the kids and teens to simply avoid the trigger if they can. Like if going to an event, seeing a particular person, playing a certain game online triggers them, avoid it by all means and you can instill that in most kids. Not all triggers are unavoidable, this is for the ones that are.

Other trigger cues can range from music, words, moods, and environment. If you are at a party or concert and the music is provocative and suggestive, the chances are that you will be, too, because it is a cue that triggers you. Same for your mood; if your household is in a depression mood, emotional fighting, or even mourning, then this, too, is cue that can trigger you. This applies for the same if you are in a toxic environment, then so will you become easily toxic thru trigger cues. The trigger words or buzzwords are if you say typically a noun, people, place, a name, it triggers, too. It's just like the ex scenario, if you say your ex name or hear somebody say it or it trending, you will get triggered immediately on cue for a response and reaction. Again, it's your choice to indulge, entertain, fuel it, or accept it and reject it as an adult of experience. However, again, this is not so with kids and teens. It's harder for them to accept it and reject it and move along. Kids cannot carry on at their early stages and phases in life and help to understand and find that equilibrium balance after spotting triggers to deal with them effectively, not to go out of hand.

Whereas, other triggers such as from suggestive body language or facial expressions set kids and teens off, too. You must be agile of these triggers, too. You cannot turn a blind eye. It's more cognitive load, mindless consumptions, and trigger habits they suffer from.

Finally the most harsh trigger that the youth suffer from is parent shaming. Most parents are undeniable and unaccountable in partaking in these type parent shaming triggers. Simply because they say it's their parenting skills and their formative way of hard press. Not realizing the actualization behind shaming their kids. Or that it triggers their kids with a negative effect. You may not see an instant reaction or response. However, it can have a huge impact on the kids from within or indirectly that manifests later on in different manners.

An example of parent shaming is a true story of this 18-year-old Tucson girl that identified as a boy, changed her name and was transgender. She was in the middle of her transition and was triggered thru shaming to commit suicide that transpired within the home. Parents shouldn't do these shaming triggers, or people within the household. You must design triggers that lead to good behaviors, outcome, and reward them. Good triggers is what kids can trigger like math, therapeutic, things to help further, and education based, etc. Remember, enjoyment is what kids will further engage in and keep them on a positive path and mindflow for positive outcome and behavior. You must put things they enjoy that they have fun and fulfillment in that they want to keep indulging in. It is to become practice, routine, then implemented into actualization and a good habit of betterment.

Again, avoid the bad triggers and embrace good triggers. Connect. Help them to transform their triggers into positive energy by recognizing the trigger before or afterwards and rechannel it. Gradually as kids and teens grow, they will grow out of certain triggers and habits with your help as a parent in proper prevention. Can you help them remove choice and just do it?

- Chapter 10 -

"Proper Prevention"

In this final chapter of prevention we will go over proper prevention, preventing poor performances as parents in this new perpetual evolving skills of keeping up with social norms and cyber influences that curves our original parenting regimen. As well as a summary of the overall focal points of previous chapters. I wrote this book's chapters in a strategic sequence to help you with framework, practical tools to shape your overall awareness, perspective, and preventive measures and actions to implement within your homes first, holding your kids accountable. Being very observant, proactive interactions, and monitoring your kids' company and content. You have all the elements and now the ingredients on how to implement your proper prevention. Let's finish up this final dialogue to spread one parent at a time to save a kid, a life, and a neighbor from home-to-home. All kids and people matter.

Let's first take a look at where we all at as time and place as humans. Also how the world has evolved and developed a digital global nervous system of advanced networks, technology, A.I. revolution, and genetic revolution that challenges who we are, what we are, Google data and algorithm choices process and decision for us. These Big Data and Tech companies have master algorithm control. Humans are now superimposed and upgraded with VR and AR. Not everybody can upgrade themselves and stay ordinary humans, lose control over their lives unmanageable. People will have a hard time connecting or keep up with this new wave shift and split of technology mediums. People's cognitive skills are deteriorating along with fundamental cognitive functions from this algorithm decision making for people's process. Whereas, the human mind and memory is becoming more dependent on A.I. to help them store, select, process things that a person is meant to do for their own cognitive health. Your mind is meant to function, not deteriorate in a blank space. It's so highly competitive with distractions from all tech, social, marketing, and the world sensitive phenoms. People can barely stick to their schedules and take time out away from the noise and stress to engage, hear self think, or other household attention and duties. An advance world with advance distractions for any typical adult, now imagine how much stress and pressure on the youth with these same worldly distractions and disconnect. Everyone is texting and limited on their time and kids' engagements. With all this new daily technology, what meaning will it give the kids and people? What will kids develop cognitive? Instant choices or process based decision influenced by those same advanced algorithms. What will they do? Especially for emotion engagement. However, there are some therapeutic VR/AR that helps them especially if they were detoxing from bad habits, substance abuse, or other social issues.

You must remember in proper prevention that the story you tell yourself and what the kids tell themselves, that is the conflict. Therefore, practice drills and steps for school shootings needs turn focus on the parents and home as a prevention awareness. It all starts with us parents and child accountability first.

Next, let's jump into habits. The first stage of every habit is a cue craving, response, and reward system and cognitive process. It's the outcome and immediate outcome. Offer why and how to problem solve in your kids. Establish new habits first before you process. Optimize for start, prime your environment and organize it. Establish new prevention awareness habit in your head prior day before start. Habits is foundation for mastery of the craft. Automate fundamentals and you can integrate prevention engaging habits, too.

The key is to become pillars of prevention with effective parenting and evolving. It should not take a crisis for a meltdown/breakdown for change. Whatever breakdown or habits can become reinforced. Do not allow your kids to put self or other people at risk. How can kids change when they have reward, or think enablers of society 63 percent of kids today do not think it's no future they have. They get depressed, pain, and suffering.

Parents must get to the real truth and deal with it. The truth is you may have to retool as a parent. Get a vision and get strong. Tell yourself the truth and get something to go for new with kids. The emotion and psychological space. Get a strategy and go to work. Be inexcusable, meet kids' needs as well as them with yours, too. Be competent as parents and give your kids the energy, turn things around, focus on home and being a great parent of proper prevention.

Change your approach and take action every day. Power of decision and choice have to get thru crisis and active. Activate your resources. People need to be aware of true identity versus not relate of what people want them to be, authentic self that's lost. Awaken them in the presence. They have a fictitious meter and sense of reality that's warped and lost. A lot of parents are exhausted and not paying attention. The attachment and achievement. Then we cut them. We looking for wholeness, validations, identities, labels. Each one of them follows archetypes. To be awake to the wholeness of present reality. Be aware of your unconscious is a reflection of your split and resistance. Therefore, trust your process as a parent and what you going thru and what your kids going thru is temporary. If you don't trust, you are resisting and giving it negative energy.

Going thru a challenge with your kids and teens and being a parent on Earth is what you're meant to do and endure. You can shift the impossible. It don't mean to resign as a person. Do not give your power away to it.

Do detailed action plans, concrete goals, personal accountability, constructive feedback, all important your parenting structure and commitment for prevention. Then enthusiasm and belief in your abilities increase exponentially. Then you become a prevention advocate and an unstoppable force for personal development, and sharing your system with other parents.

Make a huge shift in your home. Start with a slight shift and just a step to move forward progress with your proper prevention, not overnight but it will eventually work out just right.

Remember this, dear parents, prevention book is directed at altering your previous conditioned mind of parenting state, to manifestation of awareness of a new way of parenting, and new tools and strategies to approach it with an out-with-old-way and evolve with the new. Don't get crippled with fear. Also to seek help prior for kids suffering mental health.

Now let's go over some signs and traits of your kids have to their personality and action that you can recognize to deal with it proper and to counter it to help them. First you have the rebels. The rebels are motivated by present desires, want to do what they wanted to do. Resist all control, including self-control. They choose to act in a truth of freedom. Act in a trained thought. They love to "I'll show you better" wake up and think, what do I want to do today? Have a high level of engagement.

The questioners are motivated by sound reasons. Wakes up and thinks, what needs to be done today? Ask why-why-why? They can be paralyzed if they don't have perfect info or can't pick sides. Feel exhausted.

Next is the upholders are compliance, holding up rules, and motivated by fulfillment, self-efficient. Looking for parental rules beyond rules. They can be very rigid, and overwhelmed, or paranoid breaking the rules. A relentless quality thinking people should

Lastly the obligers are motivated by external accountability. External structures like being monitored, deadlines. "What's expected of me today." They say I'm a people pleaser, feel like they do not have a counterbalance to self. Like to burnout easily. Not self-steering or self-starting.

Now the question is, how can you create circumstances kids and teens can keep? Self-awareness and knowledge to know which element and tools to bring daily in your everyday life to get better. Like if your kids are hardcore gamers and stuck to gaming consoles all day excessive usage of overload. You should already have an effective solution formulated within the framework of this book and in previous chapters all those tools. Like a solution is to reduce friction and get the kids out of negative environment to do positive. Remove game console until positive results and responsible behavior patterns, also control usage time period only. Don't resist it. Again, small scale and master the art of implementation, being a creative in evolving parenting tactics to stay ahead of the curve. Master your work ethic, putting in your true work of awareness and proper prevention and optimize it exclusively. The biggest prevention question, proactively add prevention, engage in prevention, and inquiry. That should act as your checklist, not just as a question to yourself.

Being able to read your kids and teens during questioning of their facial expressions hint on their mood, emotions, and help you detect if they lying. Along with being agile for suggestive body language. Then awareness times ten, just like you did at their baby stages of life, is essential to successful. You need to be a selfless parent in proper prevention, putting your kids and teens first before work projects or social life. Remember it's your narration versus the child narration.

Finally, let's go over a review of the key components of this prevention book. You want to make sure your kids' chemical serotonin that makes you calm and relaxed as the body produces it is the stage of mind you bring them back to and physically reset. This cuts down on depression, anxiety, and fear. The inception was the clutter, brainwash, and mind pollution and ending with psychological effects. The problem is with all the new social norms and bullying, parents stop tending to kids and neglect their full responsibility until the kids turn 18 and out of the house. People emancipate their child to gaming, social media, edevices, and mental disease. Allowing gaming and cyber norms and influence to raise their kids instead. The cause is copycat syndrome of notoriety and seeking attention. The psychology behind fear and fear turned into a boiling eruption point from a snowball effect. The effect is the warp of perception from VR/AR to reality or social new norms effect. Being influenced also easy by gaming, digital world, etc.

Next, the method how to intervene and step into your kids' lives. Step up, guard their social media, cyber interaction, gaming usage, content, music they listen to and videos they watching. The formula to engage with kids and awareness, triggers, monitor, open up dialogue. Back-to-the-basics parenting skills times ten. Decoding text, body language, facial expressions, hidden apps etc. Get full access to your kids' edevices and learn from their data, too. The solution to spread message of awareness and engagement from one parent to another parent. Prevention from casualties, injuries, school alerts of massive shooting and suicide prevention to all decline. Develop a plan with all the tools, tips, and strategies of implement for proper prevention in this book to stop, manage, and respond. The healing and coping with tragedy. Turning loss into a lesson. Finally, proper prevention. Don't take what kids say for face value. Dig deeper, probe, and take time to make effort and engaging.

Again, your kids matter, all kids matter, and people matter. The old simple solutions back-to-basic concept of watching your own kids and raising them. They smarter nowadays. It starts in the home first. Dear parents, we must evolve and keep up with the times.

Finally, thank you for taking time out to read this prevention awareness book. Can you please help me spread this message of prevention that starts in the home, and every parent accountable to tend to their kids with tactics and strategies? You can share to schools for parents and organizations for preventions. Our main goal is to save lives by helping stop massive and school shootings by proper parental prevention. Let's be proactive and reverse it.

About Author

Hitachi Choparazzi is a New York City native, by the way of Omaha, who is currently incarcerated in level 5 solitary confinement in Florence, SMU-Eyman Complex, serving an illegal sentence awaiting on Supreme Court Appeal to correct his sentence with time served. The error forces him to serve 2 years extra.

He is an entrepreneur, tattoo artist turned author. Also the sole owner of Chop-a-Style Publishing and Productions, and the owner of Chatmon Sr. Literary Agency. He has written over 20 books and including scripts to pitch to Netflix. All this while he was incarcerated to start his reform act.

Founder and CEO of Billion-Dollar Blueprint and the BDB movement/youth movement, an innovator entrepreneurship where he believes everyone has their own blueprint, like everyone has their own unique thumbprint. Based on 3 core principles—Education, Elevation, and Innovation—which he teaches the youth and people how to format and discovery key. BillionDollarBlueprintmerch.com

The face of lockdown society movement along with the voice of lockdown society movement. IncarceratedLivesMovement. com #ILM #BDB

"I do this for y'all. I love y'all, rep y'all, and believe in y'all! I won't stop giving y'all all the raw stories as God bless them in my head. I have a hundred of them up there. Anybody that has a hot hand, send me samples or any comments, suggestions to my FB, IG Hitachi Choparazzi or email: orders@ chopastylepublishingllc.com Chop-A-Style Publishing LLC and Productions. TeflonLuv!"

Hitachi Choparazzi prides himself on having his own signature Chop-a-Style where he freestyles all his books. They all rhyme with innovation and original storylines. He writes prequels, sequels, trilogies, and more. Does it for the people who love to read and for all those incarcerated in state, federal B.O.P., county, and women's facilities. FB,IG,Tiktok, Twitter, YouTube-Hitachi Choparazzi

Emails: Hitachichoparazziauthor@gmail.com Billiondollarblueprintmerch.com

Chop-A-Style Publishing and Productions LLC

Other Books and Scripts by the Author

Non-Fiction

- How to Rap; The Elementary Teaching of Hip-Hop

- How To Tattoo & Start-Up Business

- How To Digital Detox

- How To Start-Up a Food Truck Business

- How To Stop School and Mass Shootings: Dear Parents

- Incarcerated Lives Matter: The Hitachi Choparazzi Blueprint

- How to Love

- The Switch: A Social Awareness Self-Help

- Nipsey Hussle Lockdown Society Dedication–Tribute

- If Trayvon Martin Could Talk; Injustice

Fiction

- The Eagle and Weasel (1-5 series kids' book)

- She Go! (urban novel)

- Reality Show 3D-HD (urban novel)

- Hot Thots (urban novel)

- Liqz (urban novel)

- Paranormal Whisper (horror novel)

- Pimp of Da Ratchets (urban novel)

- Pimp of Da Ratchets II Vegas (urban novel)

- Pimp of Da Ratchets 3 Orange is Da New Pimp (urban novel)

- Hitachi (urban novel)

- Penitentiary Pimp (urban novel)

- Weasel Society (urban novel)

- The Big Pep and Plucker Story-She Go! Prequel (urban novel)

Screenplays/Scripts

- Top Notch

- Hot Thots

- Pimp of Da Ratchets

- Weasel Society

- Million Dollar Games–A Secret Society

- The Eagle and Weasel (animation)

Billion Dollar Blueprint is a movement we challenge and inspire you to find your individual blueprint. Our mantra is "We believe everyone has their own blueprint like everyone has their own thumbprint". With these three core principles

Education

Elevation

Innovation

Hitachi Choparazzi is the founder and CEO. Orders available to support incarcerated businesses.

Orders available at: billiondollarblueprintmerch.com

www.ingramcontent.com/pod-product-compliance
Lightning Source LLC
Chambersburg PA
CBHW060244030426

42335CB00014B/1596